BASIC
ACCOUNTING *for* CHURCHES

A TURNKEY MANUAL

JACK A. HENRY

BROADMAN
&HOLMAN
PUBLISHERS

Nashville, Tennessee

© 1994
BROADMAN & HOLMAN PUBLISHERS

Printed in the United States of America

4261-45
0-8054-6145-0

Dewey Decimal Classification: 254.8
Subject Heading: CHURCH FINANCE
Library of Congress Card Catalog Number: 93-38256

Scripture quotations are from the *King James Version* of the Bible.

Library of Congress Cataloging-in-Publication Data
Henry, Jack A., 1928–
    Basic accounting for churches : a turn-key manual / Jack A. Henry
        p.   cm.
    ISBN 0-8054-6145-0
    1. Church finance—Accounting—Handbooks, manuals, etc.
    2. Accounting—Handbooks, manuals, etc.   3. Accounting—Problems,
exercises, etc.   I. Title.
    BV773.H46   1994
    254.8—dc20

                                              93-38256
                                                   CIP

To my wife, Dalphna,
for years of support while this book was just being talked about
and for her encouragement to go ahead and write it.
And to my former students who helped me "keep it simple."

Contents

Introduction 1

Part I. Getting Started... 5
   1. Money Management
   2. Receiving Funds
   3. Individual Giving Records
   4. Basic Bookkeeping

Part II. The Single Entry Bookkeeping System 47
   5. The Checking Account
   6. The Receipts Ledger
   7. The Disbursements Ledger
   8. The Control Sheet
   9. Financial Statements and Audits

Part III. Other Things to Consider..................................... 111
   10. Files and Supporting Documents
   11. Computers in the Church

Part IV. Practice Exercises 127
   Appendix A: Practice Problems
   Appendix B: Answers to Practice Problems

Introduction

Until you take time to consider the scriptural require-
ment to provide things honest in the sight of men as well
as in God's sight, you may decide that the best solution
to your bookkeeping problems is to ignore standard
accounting procedures and just expect people to accept
your personal honesty and good intentions when it
comes to handling, managing, and accounting for God's
money. However, once you realize that God says you
can't "cop out" so easily, you have to learn to manage
God's money in such a way as to honor Him and protect
the good name of His church and His people.

This book is written especially for the new pastor, or
one who is going out to start a new church. However, it
is also appropriate for the experienced pastor with little
or no training in financial management and bookkeeping. A background in math, accounting, or bookkeeping
is not required. A young pastor who is starting a new
church must have his time free for visitation, evangelism,
Bible study, and prayer. The procedures taught in this
book will not be excessively time consuming in day-to-
day operation and will allow the maximum amount of

time for the other duties of the ministry. They will, however, provide the young pastor and church with the ability to give a proper accounting to the whole world of how God's money is used in God's work in that church.

Although budgeting and spending are vital functions of money management, they are not directly addressed in this book. Learning to use the financial records and reports demonstrated in this book is your first priority when establishing a sound church financial management system. After the records are instituted and contain accurate and adequate information, meaningful and practical budgets and spending procedures can be developed. Take one step at a time, and do first things first.

It's Easy!

In over twenty years of teaching basic bookkeeping and business administration to future pastors and missionaries, I've found the biggest problem many students face when considering financial management is a "fear of the figures." Because they don't know the meaning of some of the jargon used by accountants, and because standard accounting reports are often printed in a form they aren't familiar with, they don't understand what the numbers they see in those reports are telling them. Because the reports are not meaningful to them, they decide the reports are useless and ignore them—and thereby take their first step toward church financial disaster.

Basic arithmetic is the highest level of math that is needed for maintaining complete, accurate, and adequate financial records that are "honest in the sight of all men." There is nothing magical about keeping records of financial income and expenditures—if you can add and subtract, you can "keep books." The church financial records are nothing more than a history, written in numbers, of the financial operation and status of the church.

Reports are for the purpose of conveying meaningful information. Money comes in and is added to the bank balance; money goes out and is subtracted from the bank balance. When you want to tell the church how much money came in and where it came from, and how much money was spent and for what, you prepare a report. You merely decide how to tell the story of the financial activity of the church so that your readers (congregation) can understand it.

Gathering the information from the church financial records for the purpose of giving a report to the church can be time consuming. However, if you organize your financial records so that numbers are grouped together that are going to be reported together, you can save yourself a significant amount of time.

The bookkeeping records outlined in this book help you keep your numbers grouped together so that preparing your financial reports can be done effectively in a minimum amount of time. Computers can provide help in a wide variety of ways in the operation of your church—small or large. The bookkeeping and accounting procedures outlined here are readily adaptable to computer accounting systems and will prove to be a major asset when understanding and using any computer accounting program.

Some things you should consider when deciding to buy a computer and/or computer accounting software are discussed in chapter 11 in order to save you hours of frustration and many dollars of the church's money as you decide what to buy and how to use it.

In appendix A, I have included practice problems for chapters 5 through 9. These problems are designed so that you actually "do" bookkeeping and participate in the physical and mental activity that bookkeeping entails. By working these problems you will become aware of the ease with which you can record and maintain the financial information you and your church need in order to get the most from the financial resources God gives you. In order to work the problems, stop by your local stationary store and buy half a dozen sheets of twenty-four-column ledger paper—that's all you need to get started. (Note: I've also included an appendix B that has the answers to the practice problems in appendix A.)

Once you have read the entire book and worked through all of the practice problems, you should be able to set up your own set of books for your church and keep them current and accurate without subtracting substantially from the time you want to spend on ministry. Relax, and don't make an easy job difficult. Remember—keep it simple but adequate.

PART ONE

Getting Started

1 Money Management / 7

2 Receiving Funds / 13

3 Individual Giving Records / 27

4 Basic Bookkeeping / 37

Pastors and churches very seldom have large amounts of money, but they often control large amounts that have been given by others for God's work. Sometimes pastors and churches excuse their disorganized and inept handling of money by saying, "The people may not understand, but God knows my heart." God tells us that it is not enough to be honest in God's sight; we must be honest in the sight of all men when it comes to handling God's money.

Seest thou a man diligent in his business?
he shall stand before kings;
he shall not stand before mean men.
— Proverbs 22:29

1

Money Management

Investing God's money while waiting to spend it is a matter that deserves careful consideration, but is not the topic of this chapter or this book.

Money management is the art and science of developing and carrying out a spending plan.

Although you may sometimes be blessed with a substantial amount of money that you have accumulated for a project and need to invest while waiting to spend it on the project, you (that is, the church) are not in the investment business. Your need to invest is only a short-term situation that may arise periodically, and it stems from not having performed your main purpose for having the money in the first place—spending it.

In this book, when speaking of money management, I will be talking about receiving, recording, budgeting, and spending money. In fact, for purposes of this study, I will define money management as the art and science of developing and carrying out a spending plan.

You will note in this definition of money management that we call it both an art and a science. The word "art" implies a degree of creativity which is necessary when developing a spending plan; the word "science" denotes the systematic way in which the spending plan is developed and operated. Both are necessary in order to get the most results from the resource in question—money. Lack of good money management is one of the biggest stumbling blocks in churches and in personal lives. The problem with most churches (and individuals) is not that they don't have enough money, but that they don't manage it well. You can get more done for less if you are a good money manager.

Lack of good money management is one of the biggest stumbling blocks in churches and in personal lives.

Relationship of Money Management Functions

The functions of money management will be treated separately in this book in order to demonstrate simple, straightforward methods associated with each one. However, they are interdependent and must be treated that way in actual practice. The practice problems in part 4 are designed to help you understand these relationships while actually performing the operations associated with each function.

The functions of money management include the following.

Receiving: the actual physical receiving of the money: counting it, safeguarding it, and preparing it for deposit in the bank.

Recording: creating the physical records that show the source and amount of income; where it is kept; how much is available; and the purpose and amount of expenditures.

Budgeting: making decisions about what to do with available income and developing a plan to implement those decisions.

Spending: the "outgo" side of money management just as receiving is the "income" side. Procedures for the actual spending of money are the consideration here.

All of the functions are vital to the effective and efficient management of church funds. If the offering is not handled carefully, not only will it be possible to lose money, but personal reputations may also be endangered. If the offering is not properly counted and cared for, the accurate recording of income is impossible. Counting errors can lead, in turn, to mistakes in budgeting. Of course, mistakes in budgeting based on erroneous records of income can lead to mistakes in spending because the spending plan will be either too optimistic or too pessimistic. Spending mistakes can bring reproach on the name of Christ and the church if they represent overspending; or they can lead to lost opportunities for growth in ministry if they represent underspending. Counting money, keeping books, planning the budget, and writing checks are all vital functions of money management and depend on each other.

Money Management and Net Worth

Net worth is an accounting term that simply means "how much you are worth." It is the sum of all that you own (cash, bank accounts, real estate, pews and pulpit furniture, folding chairs, etc.) minus all that you owe (mortgage, accounts payable, etc.). The more "what you own" exceeds "what you owe," the more you are worth—or, the greater is your net worth.

When property or equipment is purchased, money is not "spent" but is merely converted into a different form of asset. The "net worth" of the church remains the same, even though money has been removed from the checking account and is not available for spending on ministry. (If the money had been spent on ministry or expenses, the net worth would have gone down because you would have decreased the amount of your assets instead of converting them from one form to another.)

When money is managed effectively and efficiently, there is less "wastage"; the church's funds go farther toward achieving goals. More money is available for investing in assets (buildings, furniture, equipment). In either event, whether directly because of planning, or indirectly as a result of efficient operations, net worth is affected by money management.

The visible impact of good money management can also affect the amount of money available to manage. When people see their money being handled wisely and frugally so God can bless it, they are encouraged to give more, or more often, for more projects. There may also be a spiritual impact as your people recognize God's presence in their day-to-day lives when they see Him blessing the money they give. This spiritual impact may very well stimulate a growth in individual faith—which may result in growth in some ministry of the church.

That is the objective of every work of the church, including the financial management work.

Although bankers and accountants like to see a substantial figure under the "Net Worth" heading, net worth is *not* the primary measure a church should use in judging its effectiveness or its efficiency in managing its money. Remember that your church is a spending organization, organized and operated to perform a service and not to make a profit or accumulate financial assets. You receive a special offering for missions so that you can give it away to missionaries (spend it). The same could be said for your other special offerings for ministries. Missions and ministry mean "spending"; growth in net worth means growth in assets—money and things you own.

You need to own some "things," and the larger you grow, the more "things" you will need to own in order to carry out your ministry. However, the balance between the amount of your church's income that goes into assets (net worth) and the amount that is spent on missions and ministry is a visible demonstration of your church's understanding of its mission.

You must also keep in mind that the balance between growth in net worth and spending is not static. In years when you are in building or refurbishing programs, you should expect the balance to shift towards increased net worth. After all, you will probably take special offerings for the express purpose of building buildings or buying equipment, both of which are investments in assets.

When your buildings and equipment are paid for, the major share of all of your income is available for "spending"—giving to those special missions projects you have opportunity to be part of, or starting that new ministry in your community you could not afford until now. What is right for your church this year may vary from what was right last year. That is a judgment call—and you are the judge.

> Your church is a spending organization that is not expected to make a profit.

Summary

While your church is a spending organization, remember that you must receive money before you can spend it. You must record how much you receive and spend in order to know how much you have left to spend. If you plan your spending based on your planned income, you will spend your available money on the things that are most important to your ministry. Those ideas are just common sense, but they are the heart of money management—receiving, recording, budgeting, and spending.

Good money management will make it possible to buy things that have long-lasting value like buildings and land. Money spent on buildings, land, and equipment is really not "spent," but is merely invested in other kinds of assets. Converting money assets into other types of assets that are necessary to carry on the various ministries of your church, instead of spending it on expenses of ministry, preserves your net worth. A substantial net worth is considered to be a good sign in the business world, and is not wrong for a church. However, a church's net worth should not be its primary measure of good financial stewardship. You and your church must balance how you spend and invest your financial resources to accomplish the particular mission God has assigned to you.

For to their power, I bear record, yea, and beyond their power they were willing of themselves;
Praying us with much entreaty that we would receive the gift, and take upon us the fellowship of the ministering to the saints.

— 2 Corinthians 8:3–4

2

Receiving Funds

We must always remember that we receive offerings as a part of worshiping the Lord. The Word commands, the Holy Spirit moves, and the people give. The money we receive in the church offering is unlike any other money. It represents obedience and love of God on the part of His people. It also is God's method of involving His people in the work of His ministry. Because these funds are so special, although sometimes small in dollar amount, we must take special care to see that their receipt, recording, and safekeeping are done properly.

Most of the time we take for granted that "anybody can take the offering." After all, "anybody can pass the plate." We seldom think about how the plates get there to begin with so they can be passed, or what the ushers are going to do with the offering after they have passed the plates.

If you have done much traveling and visited different churches, you have undoubtedly had the experience, at least once, of having the pastor announce that it is time to receive the offering and then discover the offering plates are not in their usual place. The ushers cause a mild commotion while looking for the plates or any-thing else they can pass that will hold the offering. Usually a small cough from the preacher and a dry joke about missing offering plates accompanies the commo-tion. In the end the offering is taken, but an undesirable lesson is graphically taught to the congregation. The lesson is that the offering is such a minor part of worship, no planning or forethought is needed to accomplish it.

The offering is important to God and to His people, so we have a responsibility to see that it is received and handled properly.

The offering is important to God and to His people, so we have a responsibility to see that it is received and handled properly. In this chapter we will discuss how to physically receive the offering, count it, and provide for its physical security.

General Guidelines

1. Offering Containers

There is no set rule that says that you should use plates rather than baskets, or sacks on a pole. What you want is a container that will hold the offering and does not detract from its purpose. When starting a new church you may not have the money to buy new brass offering plates, but whatever you use should be appropriate.

If you use metal or wooden offering plates, be sure there is something in the bottom of the plate to deaden the sound of coins being dropped into the plate. Chil-dren soon learn to drop in each penny separately so they can hear the sound of it striking the plate, and so they can draw the looks of everyone in their vicinity.

Whatever kind of container you use, make sure that a sufficient quantity of them are in their proper place before each service, and that your ushers know where they are.

2. Ushers

Select and train the ushers who are going to take the offering. They should know where the containers are, your plan for taking the offering, and what to do with it after they have collected it. At special services, when you plan to do things in a special way, be sure your ushers know about all changes that affect their duties.

Notification.—You should notify your ushers in ad-vance when they are scheduled to usher. Any simple schedule will do so long as all ushers know where it is posted. If you require your ushers to wear a coat and tie, but most of your men don't dress that way on hot summer nights, neither you nor your ushers will be embarrassed by not having anyone present in proper attire if you simply schedule your ushers.

Training.—Teach them the "what" and "how" of everything you expect of them. Tell them what you want them to wear and what you want them to do. Tell them how you want them to proceed down the aisle and how to pass the plate. Do you want them to speak to everybody on the aisle and thank each one who puts something into the offering plate, or would you rather they not speak as they pass the plate? If your church is an old established church and you like the way the ushers now receive the offering, then leave it alone. However, if you are just starting, you should assume that your ushers know nothing about taking the offering.

If your church is new, your facility may have only one aisle and it may be a very short one. One man may be able to take care of both sides of the aisle by himself. If you have a larger facility, it may have two or three aisles and the aisles may be long enough that you need to divide the ushers into two or three pairs in the same aisle so they don't take an excessive amount of time to pass the offering plates to everyone present.

Whatever way your meeting room is arranged, decide how you want your ushers to position themselves before they begin and which section you want each usher to be responsible for. Show them how you want them to move in the aisle and how to pass the offering plate. Remember that there are many different ways to do any job; if you don't show them what you mean, their way may not be what you had in mind. Remind them to watch each other and stay together as they move up or down the aisle. It looks much better and is another little mark that distinguishes between good and merely satisfactory.

Let them practice a time or two so they get the "feel" of what they are doing. That way it will not seem awkward to them when they do it for the first time in a church service.

Positioning the ushers.—Let your ushers know in advance when you want them to come down the aisle. There is no reason why your entire congregation must sit quietly and wait for your ushers to come down the aisle to their assigned places. This time is wasted and interrupts the worship service. Decide ahead of time when you are going to take the offering and tell your head usher. (If

3. Receiving the Offering

15

you only have one usher, it's even easier.) If you are going to take the offering immediately after the congregation sings hymn #375, tell him, "Come down the aisle at the beginning of the fourth verse of hymn #375." By the time the congregation has finished singing the fourth verse, the ushers are in their place to take the offering, and you are ready to pray.

Another way of accomplishing the same thing is to have your ushers wait at the rear of your auditorium until you tell them to come forward. You can then use the time they take to come forward to teach a lesson about tithing and giving, or about missions.

Passing the plate.—The ushers should then pass the offering plates as you have taught them. Be observant. If some procedure needs to be changed, talk to your ushers and change it.

4. Counting the Offering

After passing the plates, make sure the ushers take the offering immediately to a secure place which has been previously designated. This place should be a room that normally does not have people going in and out during the Sunday School or worship service time. You may want to use the church office and just make it "off-limits" during the time the money is being counted. The place should allow space for spreading out the money from the offerings so that it can be counted and recorded without the counters being interrupted. Adding machines, coin wrappers, proper forms for recording the offering, and bank deposit slips all should be in place in the designated counting room before the offering is taken.

5. Securing the Funds

Securing the funds means making them safe from theft or loss by any means. Of course, the safest place to keep the offering money after it has been counted is in the bank. You should make arrangements with your bank for making "after hours deposits," so you don't have to leave the Sunday receipts in the church building overnight. If the Sunday morning offering is especially large, or you have advertised widely that you are taking a special offering for some purpose, it may be wise to take the money to the bank immediately after it has been counted in the morning instead of waiting until after the evening service. Thieves read the church page too, and are sometimes enticed by the prospects of a large sum of money being kept in a place that traditionally has very little security.

Some large churches take their offerings to the bank in locked bank bags before they are counted. In these cases, arrangements are made in advance with the bank for the bags to remain unopened until church personnel arrive at the bank on Monday morning. The funds are then counted at the bank in a room provided, deposit slips are completed by the church counters and validated by the bank, and the entire counting and deposit process is done in the secure facilities of the bank.

There should be at least two people with the offering at all times until it is counted, recorded, and secured or deposited. Having two people present does two things: it protects the funds, and it protects the reputations of the people handling the funds. There is a much smaller chance of embezzlement when two people are present because theft would require that they conspire together. By the same token, their reputations are protected because they are witnesses to each other's honesty.

In small churches where there is no separate room in which to count the offering, you may want to have the offering plates brought to the front of the auditorium and left in front of the pulpit. This is a relatively secure place because it is in plain view of everybody. If you do that, don't forget to pick it up immediately after dismissing services so it can be counted and kept in a safe location until deposited. In many churches, the offering at the mid-week services is small. The offering is usually counted and recorded, but is kept at the church and not deposited until the following Sunday when it is included in the total receipts for the day. This is a satisfactory arrangement, but you must insure that the funds are kept in a secure location while they remain at the church.

"Secure locations" in many churches are not secure. A locked drawer in a file cabinet that is accessible to several people is not secure. Putting anything else in the same drawer as the cash means people will have access to the funds who should not have. A locked toolbox-sized container may deter somebody from removing the contents, but the entire container may easily be taken from the premises so it is not a secure place.

If your church cannot afford a fireproof safe that is heavy enough to make it difficult to remove from the

> There should be at least two people with the offering at all times until it is counted, recorded, and secured or deposited.

premises, at least provide a file cabinet which can be locked, affords some fire protection, and can be chained to a permanent fixture in a manner that makes it difficult to remove. Do not put anything else in the drawer you use to store the offering. You can never provide 100 percent security, but you should plan to provide the best you can.

You can never provide 100 percent security.

6. The Pastor and Money Handling

General Rule.—It is best if the pastor never touches any cash that belongs to the church. He may act as one of the signers of checks if the checking account requires two signatures, but he should not handle cash. The reason for this rule—which should never be broken—is to protect the good name of the pastor. The first accusation usually made against any pastor by a disgruntled church member is that he probably "has his hand in the collection plate." If the procedures of the church are such that the pastor never handles cash under any circumstances, and everybody in the church knows it, then the accusations of the disgruntled member become a witness against the member instead of the pastor.

The pastor must always teach new workers how to do the job properly and the reasons for each procedure. Many pastors and laymen leave themselves open to false charges regarding theft or mishandling of church funds because they bypass some seemingly minor procedural steps (like having two people present to count the midweek offering that is traditionally only a small amount). These steps are often the ones that help protect the reputation of the person handling the funds, but the new worker will not know that unless someone teaches him. The pastor must guard his people—including their reputations.

Checking Accounts.—When a church is first started, the pastor often opens a checking account at the bank for the church and becomes the only signer on the account. This means the pastor is taking the offering, counting the money, depositing it, and signing the checks. Since his wife may be the only other member of this new congregation, and she probably isn't going to complain, this form of financial operation can be tolerated during the infant church stage, but the procedure should be changed as soon as possible. As trustworthy people join the church who are capable of receiving, counting, and recording the offerings, they should be put into service.

Personnel.—The people who count the money and record the amount received should be different from the ones who do the bookkeeping and write the checks. This procedure gives added protection to both the funds and the good name of everybody involved in the money processing of the church. For example, if the ushers collect and count the money, the church treasurer may do the bookkeeping. In some churches the ushers collect the money, the treasurer and his assistants count it, and a church financial secretary keeps the books. In all circumstances, the ones who handle the cash (receive it, count it, and deposit it) should be different from the ones who keep the books.

It may seem that I make too great an issue of protecting the funds and the good names of your people. However, Richard Bergstrom's article, "Stunned by an Inside Job," in the Winter 1987 issue of *Leadership* magazine should dispel all doubt about the importance of the procedures. Your procedures should remove all opportunities for temptation to entice your people, and provide positive evidence of their integrity.

Forms.—The rule of thumb should be to keep the record form as simple as possible while insuring that all desired information is included (see fig. 2.1). Every church is different, and every pastor's desire for information may be different. Some churches will have only a general fund offering and missions fund offering. Others may have several different offerings: general fund, missions fund, building fund, camp fund, sinking fund, etc. Some pastors may only be interested in the totals given for the day in each fund, while others may want to know when it came in, Sunday School or church, and how much each Sunday School department and class gave.

You may want to keep more than one type of record because of the varying amount of information desired for different purposes by different people. Figure 2.2 shows a "Quick Count" card that only shows totals. This may suffice for the pastor's needs on Sunday and for the needs of the bookkeeper, but would not contain all of the information the pastor may like to have when he is planning the annual missions conference and missions

7. Written Records

The people who count the money and record the amount received should be different from the ones who do the bookkeeping and write the checks.

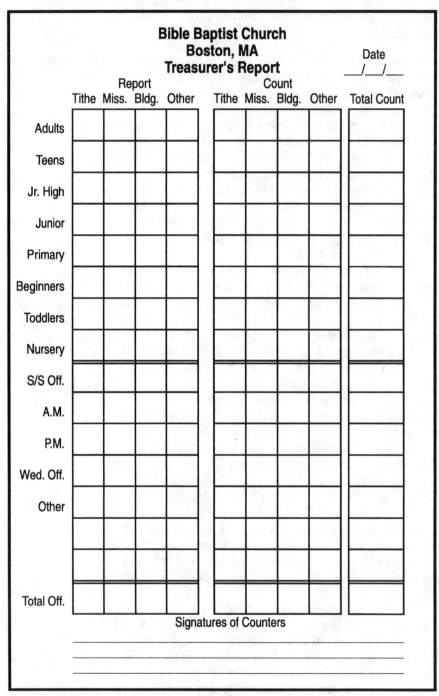

Fig. 2.1. **Treasurer's Report.** This report is used to consolidate all financial information for the weekly income.

budget. The "Treasurer's Report" form in figure 2.1 serves as a source document for many different kinds of reports that contain less information, and as a computer input or audit document if you are keeping your Sunday School records on the computer.

In this age of computers and copy machines, easy-to-use computer programs make it easy to design and produce your own forms to suit your individual needs.

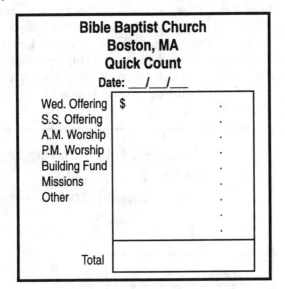

Fig. 2.2. Quick Count Report. This report may be used by the pastor when only preliminary information is available, or by the church bookkeeper after the final count has been made and validated.

Figure 2.1, Treasurer's Report, is an illustration of how a simple form that can be completed by your Sunday School workers and church ushers (or other money counters) can provide complete information about the sources of your church gift income. It also provides for recording the source and amount of other income that may be received. Figure 2.2 shows how you might use a shorter and simpler form for special purposes when complete information is not needed. Your own special requirements should determine the design of the forms you use. By producing your own forms, you can change them anytime you need to, without expensive redesign costs or wasted forms.

The rule of thumb should be to keep the record form as simple as possible while insuring that all desired information is included.

The record in figure 2.1 consolidates information from all Sunday School departments as well as the plate offerings from the church services and miscellaneous offerings. You may wonder, "Where does that information come from?" One way to generate that information is shown below, but use your own initiative and creativity in producing source documents for your specific needs.

The information you want may be captured by having each Sunday School teacher fill out a simple form such as shown in figure 2.3 and send it to his or her department superintendent, along with the class's offering envelope, during the Sunday School hour. The department superintendent then consolidates all of the forms from each class in his department and completes a departmental report showing the total for the department. That report might look something like figure 2.4. The Department Report form (fig. 2.4) that is sent to the Sunday School superintendent then provides the basis for the information contained in the Treasurer's Report, figure 2.1.

Fig. 2.3. **Class Report.** Completed by the teacher of each Sunday School class. (If not using class divisions, this should be assigned to the smallest subdivision for which you desire to gather information.)

Bible Baptist Church
Boston, MA
Class Report

Date:	
Name:	
Teacher:	

Attendance		Offering	
	Members	Tithe	$.
	New Visitors	Missions	.
	Visitors	Building	.
	Total Attend	Other	.
		Total Off.	$.

The forms from the Sunday School classes can be clipped to the Department Report (fig. 2.4) to retain the added information they contain that is not found in the consolidated reports. Inexpensive computer programs are available that will record all of this type of information for future use, and the simple forms shown here serve as ideal source documents for input into these computerized record systems. If you don't use a computer, then clip together each week's Department Reports with their class reports attached, and file them sequentially, by date, in your central office file.

Bible Baptist Church **Boston, MA** **Department Report** Date: ___/___/___			
Department			
Superintendent		Total Attendance	
Regular Offering	$	Visitors	
Mission Offering	$	First-Time Visitors	
Building Fund	$	Personal Calls	
Other	$	Phone Calls	

Fig. 2.4. **Department Report.** Form used by each Sunday School department.

To safeguard the funds during all of this money handling, each class envelope containing money should be sealed by the teacher and the Class Report attached to the outside before sending it to the department superintendent. There is no need to validate the amounts marked on the class envelopes at the department level because that will be done by the church counters when they consolidate the entire Sunday School offering.

Note that the church record, figure 2.1, has two columns for entering the Sunday School offering for each department, "Report" and "Count." The "Report" column shows the amount reported on the department report, and the "Count" column shows the amount actually counted by the church counters. This procedure is convenient if counting the Sunday School offering is postponed until after the morning services. The "Report" amount makes it possible to know approximately how much the offering was in Sunday School even though it has not been officially counted. Since, in many churches, the major portion of the total offering is received in the Sunday School, this gives the pastor information he may want to report to the church during the worship service.

If there is a difference between the "Report" and the "Count" columns, the church counters should reverify their count before entering it. The "count" amount is considered to be the correct figure. If there were individual giving envelopes in the class envelope, and one of those had an error in the amount shown on the outside of the envelope, then that would cause a difference between the "Report" column and the "Count" column. If not, then simple arithmetic is probably the cause of the difference between the two columns.

There is also a place on figure 2.1 for the people who count the offering to sign their names. This is important in maintaining complete records. If the bank deposit is often in error after certain teams of counters have counted the offerings, you may need to provide them with more training or some incentive to be more accurate. Also, you must realize that in today's society not all adults are able to count accurately or do simple arithmetic. In this case, you may need to make some changes in your people who count the money. You will want to do this discreetly so that you do not embarrass anyone, but you must do it in order to have accurate church records.

Bank Deposit.—When the money is all counted and appropriate entries are made in the report forms, the bank deposit slip should be prepared. Completing this deposit slip is covered in chapter five.

8. Counting Money

General.—Make sure your money counters do not miss the worship services in order to count the offerings. They need the spiritual food too. If the Sunday School offering cannot be counted before the worship service begins, then do it afterward. If counting the "plate offering" is going to cause missing the preaching, then secure the funds and count them later. The general rule is to count the offerings as soon as possible after receiving them, but do not miss church.

Handling Envelopes.—Many churches have an envelope system for individuals to use in their systematic giving to the church.